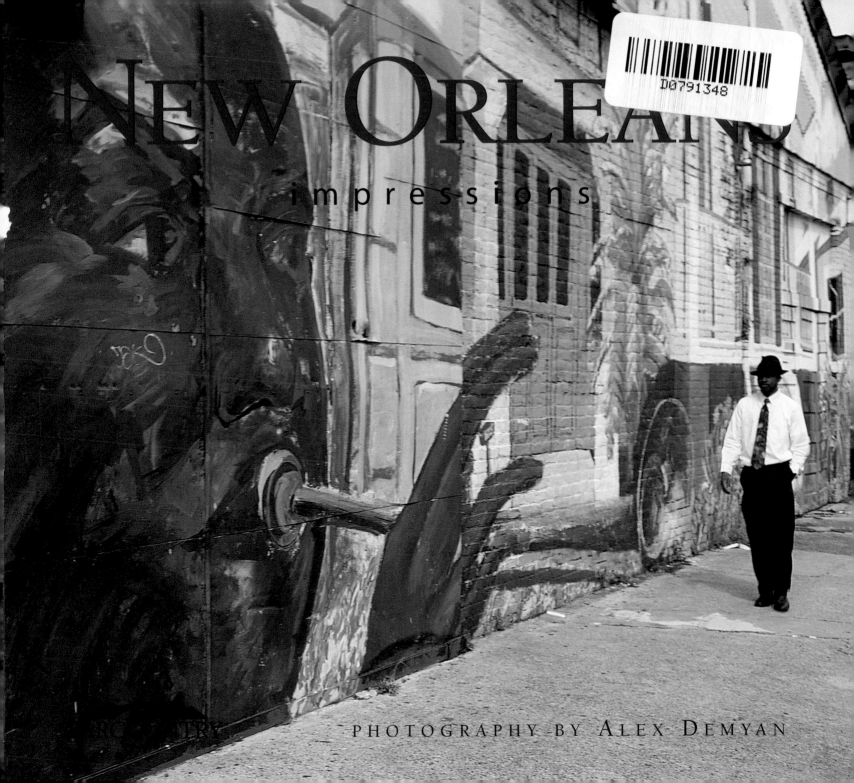

NEW ORLEANS

impressions

PHOTOGRAPHY BY ALEX DEMYAN

Title page: The Praline Connection Gospel and Blues Hall in New Orleans' Warehouse District serves up some of the city's finest down-home Cajun-Creole soul food. Although there's no live music during the week, on Sundays it offers the most spirited brunch in town.

Right: Like two diamond bracelets spanning the Mississippi River, the bridges that connect downtown New Orleans with Algiers are located at a section of the river where it actually flows north before winding south into the Gulf of Mexico.

Front cover: During the day, Jackson Square is the gathering place for tourists, artists, fortune tellers, tarot card readers, and mule-drawn carriages. By night, deserted and muffled by a soft rain and heavy fog, it becomes dreamlike and mysterious.

Back cover: A characteristic wrought-iron balcony on Dauphine Street in the French Quarter is silhouetted by a cloudless sunset.

ISBN 1-56037-364-4
Photography © 2005 by Alex Demyan
© 2005 Farcountry Press

For more information about our books write Farcountry Press, P.O. Box 5630, Helena, MT 59604; call (800) 821-3874; or visit www.farcountrypress.com.

Created, produced, and designed in the United States.
Printed in China.

09 08 07 06 05   1 2 3 4 5

Lots of locals think of Lake Pontchartrain as their own private backyard fishing hole. Among the most plentiful species are sheepshead and speckled trout.

Beware of New Orleans, for it can be seductive—luring the unsuspecting visitor into its web of sensations and overcoming them with sights, tastes, sounds, and even fragrances—be they from tropical vines or from steaming pots filled with native seafood and tangy spices. Suddenly, guests will find themselves enamored with the Crescent City, nicknamed as such because of the crescent-shaped landform—created by the serpentine Mississippi River—on which the city has developed.

Poets, writers, and artists have been particularly vulnerable to New Orleans' appeal. Writer Tennessee Williams became smitten and returned to the Crescent City often. Others never left, including photographer Alex Demyan, whose images grace this book. As a young man from Mansfield, Ohio, Demyan decided, in 1975, that New Orleans was where he wanted to stay. Here his art found him, as he developed an interest, and then an expertise, in photography—driven by the desire to chronicle the life that flowered around him.

One of the first things one associates with New Orleans is its rich musical heritage. And this thriving music scene was not created by a big bang—rather it evolved. That evolution began in New Orleans where musicians, freed from the restraints of classical training and far enough removed from the mainstream to be inhibited by it, began improvising. Blues, gospel, and ragtime were part of the mix from which came a sound like no other. It was songs of the streets that were played, in the early days, mostly by the city's poor and outcast citizens—particularly those of African and Sicilian descent. And the Mississippi River and the railroads provided channels through which the music could flow.

Serving as the source of the music was, itself, a mighty contribution, but New Orleans stirred in another element—Louis Armstrong, one of jazz's greatest performers. Armstrong gave jazz a face and a personality. In 1949 Armstrong, by then an international star, returned to New Orleans to serve as king of the Zulu Parade. His hometown had long mastered the art of celebration. Its carnival and that of Rio de Janeiro are the largest in the world. Quirky elements of the New Orleans style of Mardi Gras include the use of the specially created moniker "krewe" to describe carnival organizations, the custom of throwing trinkets from floats, and the bright colors of purple, green, and gold. Those traditions are often imitated by other communities—though none possesses the history and know-how of the city of New Orleans.

Then there's the custom of serving "king cake"—a pastry in which one slice contains a hidden object, usually a plastic baby—in celebration of the Twelfth

Below: In 1803, the Louisiana Purchase was signed over to the United States at The Cabildo in the French Quarter. Today, it houses family-friendly exhibits of life in Louisiana.

Foreword

by **Errol Laborde,** editor
New Orleans Magazine
and *Louisiana Life Magazine*

Night. The person who draws the loaded slice becomes king or queen of the occasion—even if the occasion is just coffee in the office lunch room.

In theory, Mardi Gras (French for "Fat Tuesday") is supposed to represent the last day of fasting before Ash Wednesday and the solemn period of Lent that follows. But New Orleanians are far more adept at feasting than fasting. Abstinence from meat might be satisfied, for example, with an oyster poor-boy: the fried bivalves are placed between slices of toasted, buttered French bread and garnished with lettuce, tomato, lots of catsup, and perhaps a twist of lemon.

New Orleans is blessed by its culinary heritage, the major influences of which are French, Creole, Caribbean, African, and Sicilian, with touches of spice from the nearby Cajun country. The Gulf of Mexico, Lake Pontchartrain, and the estuary systems of the Atchafalaya Basin are generous in their supply of seafood.

As a tourist destination the Crescent City is certainly a medalist, constantly ranked as one of the most popular travel destinations. It is a compact city with many of its main attractions within walking distance of Canal Street, the town's main thoroughfare. The most historic part of the New Orleans is the French Quarter, home of not only bawdy Bourbon Street but elegant old buildings, some with antique shops, all of which are antiques in themselves. The historic epicenter of the Quarter is Jackson Square, in front of the St. Louis Cathedral. Formerly known as the Place d'Armes, it was here in 1803 that the Louisiana Territory was ceremoniously transferred from Napoleon's France to the fledgling United States. President Thomas Jefferson, sensing the port city's geographic importance, had meant to buy just New Orleans from the French, but cash-strapped Napoleon decided to throw into the deal the entire Louisiana Territory, reaching as far west and north as today's Montana. On the field at Jackson Square, the United States became a far-flung nation and New Orleans one of its most important cities.

Alex Demyan offers a glimpse of what makes New Orleans one of the most unique, vibrant, and eclectic places on earth. View at your own risk though, for you too might be seduced by the city.

Right: A native of New Orleans, writer Anne Rice has owned many houses in the city, including this Garden District beauty. She's active in preservation causes, and her "vampire empire" includes a tour company and a winemaking business.

Facing page: A gift to New Orleans from the government of Spain, Spanish Plaza displays coats of arms of all the Spanish provinces. Its azulejo tiles are like those at Plaza de España in Seville. The stones and fountain for the Plaza were shipped directly from Spain to New Orleans.

Right: The Hotel Monteleone, in the heart of the French Quarter, is one of the oldest in the city. Long a favorite of writers (such as Ernest Hemingway), its revolving Carousel Bar offers a bird's-eye view of activity in the Quarter.

Below: Paul Prudhomme's K-Paul's Louisiana Kitchen is a do-not-miss-stop in the French Quarter. His style of cooking led to a plethora of chefs creating heated Cajun dishes.

Right: Canal Street was once like a park, with grass and many trees. Today it is the center of the central business district and also serves as a major reference point when giving or receiving directions.

Below: A visitor is bound to see brilliant Hawaiian-print shirts, Parrotheads, and maybe even Jimmy Buffet himself at Margaritaville in the French Quarter.

Left: The West End of Lake Pontchartrain used to be called New Lake End. Louis Armstrong played at many of the lakeshore resorts; one of his most popular tunes was called "West End Blues."

Below: Flowery splashes of color, ponds, fountains, and a huge collection of mature live oaks draw visitors to the Botanical Garden in City Park.

Facing page: Café du Monde, at the gateway to the French Market and just off Jackson Square, is justly famous for its beignets (pronounced ben-YAYs, a New Orleans doughnut-like fried delight), smothered in powdered sugar, and café au lait. Grab plenty of napkins and enjoy the 24-hour-a-day scenery.

Left: The Louisiana Superdome contains no posts—except, of course, goal posts when the New Orleans Saints play there. It's as tall as a 27-story building and contains no windows.

Below: Hot sauce comes in many colors, shapes, and temperatures—from a gentle heat to a XXX-rated variety with skull and crossbones on the label.

Facing page: Magazine Street comprises six miles of galleries and shops and extends from Canal Street to Audubon Park.

Below: It's Saturday in Audubon Park and you'll see joggers, couples pushing babies in strollers, cyclists, and folks walking their dogs. Although it's near both Tulane and Loyola universities, a visitor can always find a quiet spot to watch birds or other wildlife.

Right: City Park is one of the largest urban parks in the country. It attracts more than 12 million visitors a year and spreads over 1,500 acres.

Below: Beguiling, mysterious, noisy, crowded, smelly, and captivating, the Vieux Carré (Old Square) is where New Orleans began.

Far left: Think of one and the other comes to mind: New Orleans and Dixieland jazz. Preservation Hall still offers some of the best musicians playing some of the finest traditional Dixieland jazz.

Left: The U.S. Coast Guard headquarters in New Orleans serve as a convenient and easy-to-spot landmark for watercraft on Lake Pontchartrain. The "New Orleans Group," as they are called, supervises boating safety laws and keeps the busy Port of New Orleans safe and secure.

Right: The Garden District seems like a quiet, magical setting when compared with the bold and fun-loving atmosphere of the French Quarter. A visitor can still understand why the District was *the* place to live in New Orleans' early days.

Below: Ol' Man River just keeps rollin' along. River traffic has changed, but the route from the Midwest to the Gulf still flows through the Crescent City.

Above: Faubourg Marigny invites visitors to explore an array of restaurants, bars, and nightclubs, many located along Frenchmen Street. Located at the edge of the French Quarter, it is probably the best-preserved nineteenth-century neighborhood in the city, with a striking variety of colorful Creole cottages and shotgun houses.

Right: Anything goes. Party hearty. Serious fun. It doesn't have to be Mardi Gras for Bourbon Street to exemplify the cry, "Laissez les bon temps rouler" (Let the good times roll)!

Left: Considered by many to be the oldest building in the Quarter, the Blacksmith Shop on Bourbon Street reportedly was used by pirates Pierre and Jean Lafitte to "fence" their ill-gotten, high-seas booty.

Below: Today's hitching posts are rarely used. Yet, they remain curiosities and reminders of days gone by.

Right: Formed in the 1950s, the Zeus Krewe was the first to parade in Metairie.

Left: With so many things to see and do in the Crescent City, it is possible to overlook the busy Port of New Orleans. The river-sea complex, one of the largest ports in the nation, not only accommodates barge traffic coming downriver, but also services ships coming upriver from the Gulf.

Right: The Zulu Parade, established in 1909 and one of the most boisterous of Mardi Gras, offers highly sought-after parade trinkets: decorated coconuts called "golden nuggets."

Left: Behind the noise and bustle of the French Quarter, doors open to lush gardens and rooftop views. Many people who live there wouldn't choose to live anywhere else.

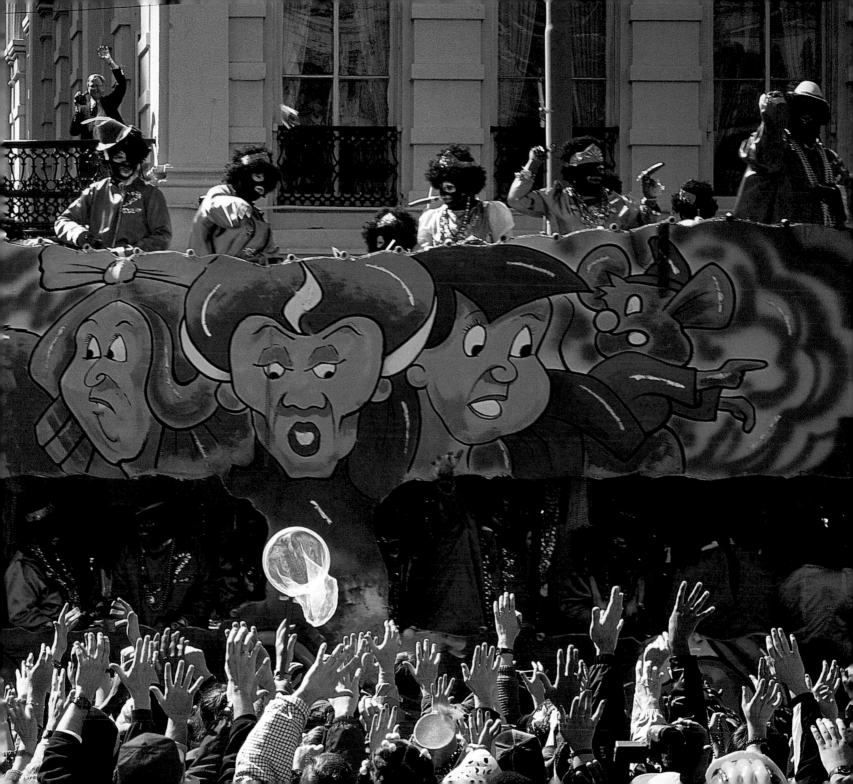

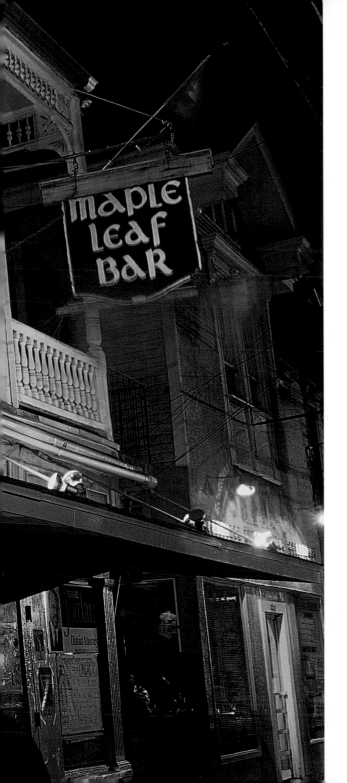

Above: Napoleon House was built as safe haven for Napoleon Bonaparte; some historians even hint at a plot to kidnap him from Elba and bring him to safety in New Orleans. Although he never made it, today's Napoleon House offers a funky, quiet retreat in the Quarter, complete with classical music playing in the background.

Left: A sweaty, overcrowded dance floor draws both locals and tourists to the Maple Leaf Bar, uptown on Oak Street. Several bands play regular sets during the week, but Sunday afternoon is reserved for poetry.

Right: Longue Vue House in Metairie is a Greek Revival mansion brimming with furnishings and other antiques from eighteenth- and nineteenth-century America and England. The mansion is surrounded by eight acres of gardens and fountains, including a half-acre interactive garden for children.

Left: Tulane University dates to 1834, when the Medical College of Louisiana was founded. It was named to honor Paul Tulane, who left $1 million to the college.

Below: Both inside and out, Pat O'Brien's on St. Peter Street in the Quarter is always jumping. Nobody questions the establishment's claim as "The Home of the Hurricane," a powerful rum potion served in hurricane lamp-shaped glasses.

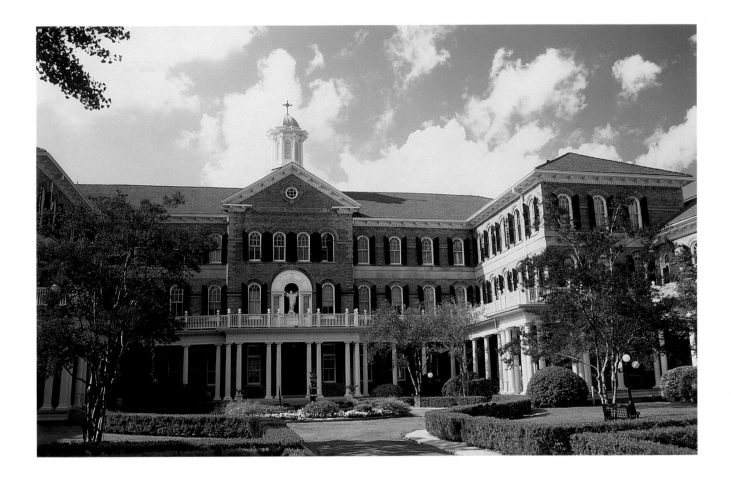

Above: The Academy of the Sacred Heart is a girls' school, pre-kindergarten through twelfth grade, founded by the Society of the Sacred Heart in 1887. The Society is an international group of academic institutions founded in France in 1800.

Facing page: Billed as the only "authentic" steamboat in New Orleans, the *Natchez* offers cruises, dining, and Dixieland jazz.

Facing page and below: Mardi Gras in New Orleans is an explosion of color, extravagant costumes, and equally extravagant behavior, with streets and balconies jammed with visitors from all over the world. Literally, it's "Fat Tuesday," and the goal is to party as much as possible before Ash Wednesday, the beginning of Lent.

For some, the connection to New Orleans is simple: jazz, and plenty of it. For others, the draw is architecture or history. The skyline gleaming like it's ready for a big party makes everybody feel welcome.

Right: Riding one of the old olive-green streetcars on the St. Charles Avenue Line is a wonderful way to become friendly with New Orleans. From Canal Street, the line runs up St. Charles, past the Garden District and the campuses of both Tulane and Loyola, and to Audubon Park.

Below: For a few months in 1861, this building had the distinction of housing the Confederacy's only mint. The building was then used as a U.S. mint until 1909. The Old U.S. Mint now houses the New Orleans Jazz Museum, where visitors can unravel the history of music in the city back to the 1790s.

Left: The opulent, grand lobby of the Sheraton Hotel on Canal Street welcomes guests to the forty-nine-story hotel. The hotel's location puts visitors within easy walking distance of the French Quarter, the Mississippi River, tantalizing shopping, and the Superdome.

Below: The Algiers Courthouse was built on the site of one of the first plantation homes in that part of the city, just across the river from Jackson Square. This Romanesque Revival building, built in 1896, is the third-oldest continuously used courthouse in Louisiana.

Right: Jackson Square is the town square in the heart of the French Quarter. Originally called Place d'Armes, it served a variety of purposes and was once used as a military parade grounds. In the 1850s, the square was named to honor Gen. Andrew Jackson, hero of the Battle of New Orleans.

Below: Originally called Fort Petite Coquilles, Fort Pike (completed in 1826) later replaced the small, wooden fort that guarded the narrow passage between Lake Pontchartrain and the Gulf of Mexico. It was named for the explorer and soldier Gen. Zebulon Pike.

Above: Fireworks over the French Quarter and the Mississippi River usher in the New Year New Orleans style—flashy, colorful, and spectacular.

Right: The Voodoo Museum, between Bourbon and Royal streets, is dedicated to Voodoo and Marie Laveau, Voodoo Queen of the city from 1796 to 1881. The museum is a mix of sacred and mysterious objects associated with voodoo magic and religion.

Facing page: The galleries and balconies along Royal Street are prime spots to catch summer evening breezes. They are also great places to watch Mardi Gras festivities. On Royal Street, the term "gallery" can also apply to one of the many art galleries along this busy thoroughfare.

Above: The Rayne United Memorial Methodist Church, on the corner of St. Charles Avenue and General Taylor Street, was built in 1875. It was named in honor of Robert W. Rayne, who paid for more than half of the construction costs to memorialize his son who was killed in the Civil War.

Facing page: Stately mansions, libraries, and churches grace St. Charles Avenue and provide a primer on New Orleans architectural styles.

Left: The Metairie Cemetery, at the intersection of Pontchartrain Boulevard and Metairie Road, is the largest of New Orleans' cemeteries. True to the city's reputation, the cemetery has legend to accompany it. A racetrack was once operated on the grounds, and a certain resident was allegedly denied admission to the track's exclusive Jockey Club. To exact his revenge, he bought the land and turned it into the cemetery. It is one of the few cemeteries in New Orleans that can be toured by automobile.

Below: Moonwalk is a great place to stroll and watch the ships and boats ply the river. Directly across from Jackson Square, it was named for Moon Landrieu, who was mayor of New Orleans when the walk was built.

Facing page: This fine canine looks right at home guarding the front entrance to a home in the Garden District. Typical of many homes in the District, it has abundant flowers and a wrought-iron fence and gate.

Below: Audubon Place is a privately owned street lined with mansions. The guardhouse at the entrance is older than any of the beautiful homes, including this stately residence.

Above: This flamboyant peacock resides at 340-acre Audubon Park, which stretches from St. Charles Avenue near Loyola and Tulane universities to the Mississippi River. The immense park contains Audubon Zoo, an eighteen-hole golf course, tennis courts, riding and jogging paths, and hundreds of centuries-old live oaks. It was the site of the World's Industrial and Cotton Centennial Exposition in 1884-85.

Left: Le Pavilion opened its doors in 1907 and was the first hotel in New Orleans to have elevators. The lobby is lavishly adorned with eleven chandeliers. Nobody ever goes to bed hungry; complimentary peanut butter and jelly sandwiches are available in the lobby in the evening.

Above: Fort Pike is one of six masonry forts built along the Louisiana coast to guard against foreign invasion. The forts were part of an effort by President James Monroe to protect strategic ports and rivers on the Atlantic and Gulf coasts.

Right: The Church of the Immaculate Conception, off Canal Street in downtown New Orleans and locally known as the "Jesuit's Church on Baronne Street," is one of the city's oldest. The Jesuit Order founded the parish in 1851.

Left: The Aquarium of the Americas in New Orleans is listed as one of the ten best in the country. The penguins, piranhas, sharks, and other sea creatures that inhabit its million-gallon displays will engage both adults and kids.

Below: The French Quarter Festival in April features free concerts in and around Jackson Square. Spoons and washboards are part of the scene, as well as vendors selling local savory delights.

Above: Founded in 1941, Rock 'n' Bowl Mid City Lanes on South Carrollton draws both locals and tourists with its unusual combination of bowling and music. The sound of pins falling in the eighteen-lane alley blends with the sound of saxophones, drums, and guitars. It doesn't take long for a bowler to start jitterbugging on his or her approach to the lane. The dancing goes on until 2 or 3 in the morning—and so does the bowling.

Right: Born in Louisiana, raised in Texas, Clarence "Gatemouth" Brown has been entertaining folks for more than fifty years with his unusual brand of blues, R&B, country, jazz, and Cajun. He's also accomplished on violin, viola, harmonica, and mandolin, and even plays the drums. He has influenced a couple of generations of musicians, from Frank Zappa to Eric Clapton. Most often, the word "legendary" appears before his name.

Facing page: Christmas in Algiers doesn't have snow, but the city shines with the glow of thousands of lights.

Above: Music is everywhere in the Big Easy. It begins early and lasts a lifetime. This young musician can follow any number of musical paths—zydeco, blues, jazz, or even win a chair with the New Orleans Philharmonic.

Right: Visitors can explore parts of Bayou Sauvage National Wildlife Refuge's 23,000 acres aboard a swamp tour boat. One of the largest urban wildlife refuges in the country, it offers nature trails, board-walks, picnic areas, fishing, boating, guided canoe trips, and bird-watching.

Facing page: Also known as the de la Houssaye House, the "Wedding Cake House," uptown on St. Charles Avenue, is a stunning example of Georgian Revival architecture. Its porticoes, decorative balconies, and beveled glass in the front door make it a perfect site for weddings, receptions, teas, and other social gatherings.

Below: The Ghostly Galavant, an annual event sponsored by Friends of The Cabildo, allows visitors to step into private courtyards in the French Quarter where some of the city's most well-known historical "ghosts" tell their tales.

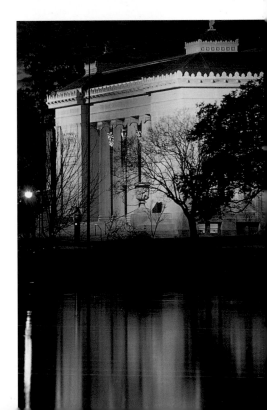

Above: There is no better way to experience New Orleans hospitality than to stay at a bed and breakfast, such as The House on Bayou Road. Visitors will learn history with a local's perspective and knowledge.

Right: City Park provides a backdrop for the New Orleans Museum of Art. The museum contains a permanent collection of over 40,000 pieces, traveling exhibits, and special displays and art scavenger hunts for kids.

Left: Arnaud's, in the French Quarter, is a long-established and highly regarded place to dine. In a beautifully restored building, it is formal and elegant. Its flickering gas lights and antique ceiling fans create a turn-of-the century feeling.

Facing page: Lakeshore Drive runs along the shores of Lake Pontchartrain in Lakeshore Park. The area is a popular place on sunny days for swimming, picnicking, and enjoying the view.

Below: Built in 1927 in the tradition of grand European theaters, the Saenger Theatre's décor is Renaissance, with Greek and Roman sculpture, marble statues, and cut-glass chandeliers.

Facing page: Wrought iron, delicate yet enduring, and balconies are two images that transport visitors to the warm spring evenings and gracious Southern living of the Garden District.

Right: The eight-acre Longue Vue estate in Metairie uses fountains, ponds, and gardens to accentuate the beautiful Greek Revival mansion. This elegant spiral staircase is part of the lavishly restored and decorated interior.

Below: Stories of World War II soldiers are retold at the National D-Day Museum on Magazine Street. A Smithsonian Institution affiliate, the New Orleans museum honors Andrew Higgins, a local boat builder whose amphibious landing craft was instrumental in winning the war.

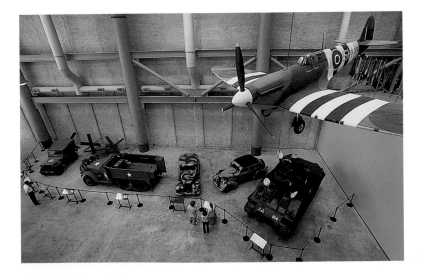

Facing page: Pirates' Alley runs between The Cabildo and St. Louis Cathedral, from Chartres Street to Royal Street. There is no historical evidence that pirates transported stolen goods along the route; however, the name is much more intriguing than the official name, Orleans Alley.

Below: The French and Spanish brought the European practice of public markets to New Orleans, a practice that still flourishes. Today's markets range from the oldest continuously running market in the nation, the French Market in the Vieux Carre, to other public and farmers' markets scattered throughout the city, such as the Crescent City Market.

Above: This girl eating beignets may have benefited from another concept that grew out of public markets, "lagniappe." Lagniappe is a practice of providing a little something extra, such as a big sprinkle of powdered sugar.

Facing page: Lake Pontchartrain is about 40 miles long and 25 miles wide. The lake has been a main waterway since the area was populated. The Lake Pontchartrain Causeway connects the city with the north shore. It is the longest bridge in the word at 23.75 miles.

Left: Built in 1884, Lee Circle honors Confederate Gen. Robert E. Lee. Holding with tradition, Lee faces north, just as he always faced the Union forces.

Below: St. Louis Cemetery #2, often called the "City of the Dead," has tombs and monuments of all sizes. Many notable people have been buried here since the 1700s, including the famous Voodoo Queen Marie Laveau.

Facing page: Not quite as famous as Preservation Hall, Maison Bourbon is just as dedicated to the tradition of showcasing Dixieland jazz. One can either enjoy the music inside the Bourbon Street bar or from the sidewalk just outside.

Right: Originally the Roosevelt Hotel, the Fairmont New Orleans is between Canal and University streets. It continues the traditions of elegance and luxury found only in "grand hotels."

Below: Louis Armstrong Park was originally the only place slaves were allowed to gather. The ground, now dedicated to the great musician, is a beautiful spot and the home of the Municipal Auditorium and Theatre for the Performing Arts.

Alex Demyan, born and raised in Mansfield, Ohio, studied journalism at the University of Missouri and then settled in New Orleans, where he has lived since 1975.

Alex recounts: "I had some basic training in photography during college, but it was only much later that the constant exposure to the photo-rich environment of New Orleans brought forth a passion to create images. From there, it was a steady progression from that first "wow" from my wife, Jill, to finding my brothers-in-law still awake after my slide shows to getting my first photograph published in 1997."

Alex turned professional in 1998 at the age of 46 and is now recognized as one of the South's top photographers.

Alex has had thousands of his images published worldwide and has received "Pictures of the Year" awards from *American Photo* and *Popular Photography* magazines.

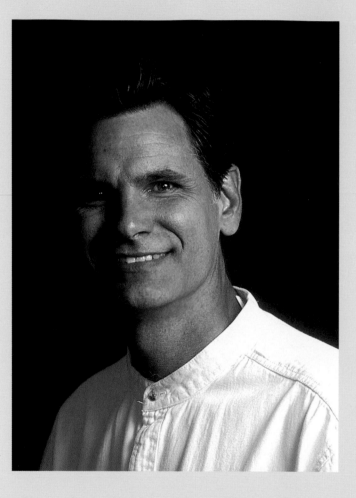